LIFE ON THE RESERVATION

💧 A Native American woman walks toward her hogan, an earth-covered dwelling, on the Navajo Indian reservation in Arizona. Life on the reservation is a delicate balance between old and new ways of life.

LIFE ON THE RESERVATION

BARBARA SAFFER

Oak Knoll Middle School Library

MASON CREST PUBLISHERS

Mason Crest Publishers
370 Reed Road
Broomall PA 19008
www.masoncrest.com

Copyright © 2003 by Mason Crest Publishers.
All rights reserved. Printed and bound in the
Hashemite Kingdom of Jordan.

First printing

1 3 5 7 9 8 6 4 2

Library of Congress Cataloging-in-Publication Data
on file at the Library of Congress

ISBN 1-59084-070-4

Publisher's note: many of the quotations in this book come from
original sources, and contain the spelling and grammatical
inconsistencies of the original text.

CONTENTS

1 **INDIANS CLASH WITH EUROPEANS**   6

2 **AMERICA ESTABLISHES INDIAN TERRITORY**   14

3 **THE LAST INDIAN UPRISINGS**   20

4 **RESERVATIONS**   30

5 **CHANGES ON THE RESERVATIONS**   40

6 **MODERN RESERVATIONS**   48

GLOSSARY   56

TIMELINE   58

FURTHER READING   61

INTERNET RESOURCES   62

INDEX   63

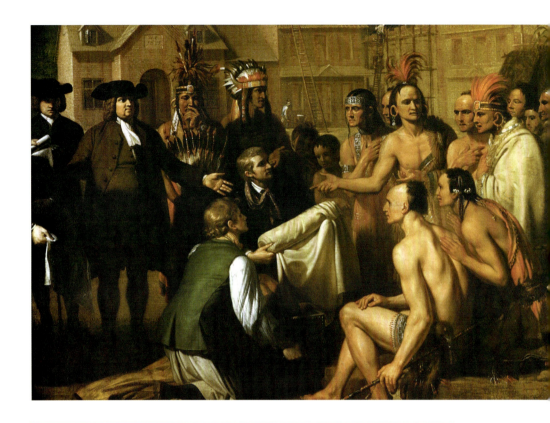

💧 William Penn, an English Quaker who founded the colony of Pennsylvania, established friendly relations with the Native American tribes of the area. Many other colonists preferred to dominate the Indians rather than deal with them as equals.

INDIANS CLASH WITH EUROPEANS

DURING THE LAST ICE AGE, A LAND BRIDGE SPANNED THE BERING STRAIT BETWEEN ASIA and North America. In pursuit of prey, **nomadic** Asian hunters crossed the land bridge, probably between 20,000 and 60,000 years ago. These travelers were the ancestors of American Indians. Over the years, the **migrants** spread across the New World. In time they formed many tribes, each with its own home region, appearance, language, and culture.

By the time Europeans began **colonizing** North America in the 1600s, 240 tribes—about one million Native Americans in all—lived on the continent. Some tribes, like the Apache, Blackfeet, Arapaho, Comanche, and Navajo, were nomadic hunters and fierce warriors. Other tribes, such as the Choctaw, Delaware, Mohave, Yuma, and Zuñi, were skilled farmers as well as hunters. And some bands, like the Kansa, Omaha, and Iowa, were migrants who slowly moved from place to place as they stalked animals and grew crops.

Soon after they arrived in the New World, the British began

8 LIFE ON THE RESERVATION

An Indian prophet named Abnaki declared that he had a message for Indians from the Great Spirit. "I give you warning," he said, "that if you suffer the Englishmen to dwell in your midst, their diseases and their poisons shall destroy you…and you shall die."

pushing the Indians off their native lands. When the first permanent English colony was founded in Jamestown, Virginia, in 1607, the colonists' dealings with the neighboring Powhatan Indians were friendly. The Native Americans helped the new settlers and gave them food. Relations broke down, however, when the colonists moved onto Indian land. Fierce battles followed, and the settlers came to hate and fear Native Americans.

The Jamestown settlers defeated the Powhatans in 1646, took their property, and forced the Indians to live on small patches of land. This confinement of Native Americans was the forerunner of the **reservation** system.

Some whites, such as Quaker leader William Penn and Rhode Island founder Roger Williams, tried to be fair to Native Americans. Williams, appalled at English treatment of the Indians, declared that even kings had no right "to take and give away the lands and countries of other men." After Williams and Penn died, however, the Indians had few European supporters.

During the 1600s, Indians fought many battles with English settlers along the east coast. The outcome was always the same. The British—who had well-organized

INDIANS CLASH WITH EUROPEANS

> The English begin constructing a fort on the James River in 1607. Their colony, Jamestown, would become the first permanent English settlement in North America.

armies with guns—defeated the Indians, who fought with spears, clubs, and bows and arrows. Afterward, the English took over Indian lands. As a result, Native Americans were pushed farther and farther west.

Being forced off their land caused the Indians great physical and mental suffering. Contact with whites exposed Native Americans to deadly European diseases, such as measles, smallpox, plague, and influenza. These diseases killed

LIFE ON THE RESERVATION

Metacomet (1638–1676) was chief of the Wampanoag Indians of Massachusetts and Rhode Island. The English colonists there called him King Philip. Metacomet was friendly with the English settlers until the colonists took over large sections of Wampanoag land and tried to impose their laws on the Indians. To halt English expansion, Metacomet organized a federation of New England tribes in 1657. The war that erupted in June 1675, when the colonists executed three Wampanoags for killing an Indian traitor, came to be called "King Philip's War." During the war, Indians smashed frontier towns, and colonists massacred Native American villages.

By 1676, Metacomet realized he was losing the struggle. His supplies were running out, many allies had deserted him, and some former confederates were helping the English. Metacomet returned to his home in Mount Hope (now Bristol, Rhode Island) with the remaining Wampanoags. On August 12, 1676 Metacomet was ambushed and shot by John Alderman, an Indian working for the English. The colonists cut off Metacomet's head and displayed it on a stake in Plymouth, Massachusetts, for the next 25 years. After Metacomet's death Indian resistance in southern New England ended, and the settlers freely expanded their settlements across the region.

INDIANS CLASH WITH EUROPEANS

👆 Chief Pontiac, a leader of the Ottawa tribe, confronts a British colonel named Henry Bouquet in 1764. Bouquet had encouraged his soldiers to spread smallpox among the Ottawa by deliberately infecting blankets, then giving them to the Indians after a meeting.

hundreds of thousands of Indians. Moreover, Europeans introduced Native Americans to alcoholic beverages, and in their despair many Indians became alcoholics.

12 LIFE ON THE RESERVATION

Pontiac (1720–1769) was chief of the Ottawa Indians, a tribe that lived near the upper Ottawa River in Canada. In 1762, Chief Pontiac organized an alliance among Native American tribes from Lake Superior to the lower Mississippi River. He hoped to halt the expansion of British settlements into the region. At an Indian assembly in April 1763, Pontiac denounced English colonists' treatment of Indians. He said the Great Spirit wanted the Indians to return to the customs and weapons of their ancestors, throw away tools obtained from whites (guns, steel axes, steel knives, animal traps, fishing nets), stop drinking alcohol, and drive out the English. "I mean to destroy the English," Pontiac told the Indians, "and leave not one upon our lands."

Under Pontiac's leadership, the Indian alliance waged "Pontiac's War" from 1763 to 1764. Overall, Pontiac's War inflicted great damage on the English. Native Americans captured eight of 12 targeted forts, slaughtered thousands of British troops, and wiped out large numbers of English settlements. He also besieged the British fort at Detroit for six months, before being forced to withdraw at the end of October 1763.

By 1764, however, many tribes were tired of fighting. Also, most Indians had become dependent on European goods and wanted to resume trading with the British. Because his allies were deserting him, Pontiac agreed to a truce with his enemies. In a 1766 peace treaty the English pledged to respect Indian property rights, but they soon broke this promise.

On April 20, 1769, while Pontiac was visiting Cahokia, Illinois, a Peoria Indian stabbed and killed him. Pontiac's death started a brutal war among the tribes, and the Peoria Indians were almost wiped out. Meanwhile, an English commander named John Wilkins, out of respect for the great warrior Pontiac, ordered the chief buried along the Mississippi River in Cahokia.

British authorities tried to halt American settlers' westward migration until agreements were forged with the Native Americans. However, the colonists, who wanted new lands, ignored British proclamations and continued to move west. Lord Dunmore, the governor of Virginia, expressed the settlers' feelings in 1774: "The [Americans]…do not conceive that Government has any right to forbid their taking possession of a vast tract of country either uninhabited or which serves only as a shelter to a few scattered tribes of Indians."

There was no easy way to resolve the Europeans' longing for land with the Native Americans' right to their homelands. Most white settlers refused to even acknowledge that the Indians' anger was justified. The tension between the two groups of people was just beginning.

In the battle of the Thames in 1811, Native Americans fought against Kentucky volunteer troops. During the fighting, Shawnee chief Tecumseh was shot in the chest. This was a tremendous loss to his tribe.

AMERICA ESTABLISHES INDIAN TERRITORY

DURING THE AMERICAN REVOLUTION, WHICH LASTED FROM 1776 TO 1783, THE BRITISH AND Americans each tried to gain Native American allies. No matter whose side the Indians fought on, though, they suffered in the end. After the colonies won the war, America's new boundaries extended from the Atlantic Ocean on the east to the Mississippi River on the west, and from Canada on the north to Florida on the south. The stage was set for Americans to take over more Indian land.

When Congress passed the Northwest Ordinance in 1787, allowing Americans to settle the Northwest Territory above the Ohio River, colonists flooded into Illinois, Indiana, Michigan, Ohio, and Wisconsin. An alliance of several tribes, led by Chief Little Turtle of the Miami Indians, fought ferociously to drive the settlers out. The Native Americans lost. They had to surrender part of the Northwest Territory to Americans.

Prodded by the federal government and hostile white settlers, many tribes surrendered their land for money, tools,

LIFE ON THE RESERVATION

> Tecumseh (1768–1813), a great warrior and public speaker, was chief of the Shawnee Indians of Ohio. When whites began moving into the Northwest Territory, Tecumseh declared, "At first, [white men] had asked for land sufficient for a wigwam; now, nothing will satisfy them but the whole of our hunting grounds, from the rising to the setting sun." To stop Indians from selling land to Americans, Tecumseh asserted, "No tribe has the right to sell, even to each other, much less to strangers… Sell a country! Why not sell the air, the great sea, as well as the earth? Didn't the Great Spirit make them all for the use of his children?"
>
> In an attempt to keep whites from taking over the Northwest Territory, Tecumseh united Native American tribes from Canada to Florida. The Indian alliance fought bravely, but crumbled when Native American forces were defeated at the Battle of Tippecanoe in 1811.
>
> After Tippecanoe, Tecumseh formed a partnership with the British, to gain military strength. In the War of 1812, between Britain and the United States, Tecumseh boldly fought alongside English soldiers. He died on the battlefield on October 1813. His death ended Indian resistance in the Northwest Territory.

trinkets, and the promise of new homes west of the Mississippi River. William Henry Harrison, **superintendent** of the Northwest Indians, was a treaty **negotiator** for the United States. In an 1810 speech Harrison defended America's Indian policy by saying: "Is one of the fairest portions of the globe to remain in a state of nature, the haunt of a few wretched savages, when it seems destined, by the Creator, to give support to a large population, and to be the seat of civilization, of science, and true religion?"

AMERICA ESTABLISHES INDIAN TERRITORY

The Shawnee chief, Tecumseh, was infuriated by Harrison's growing demands for land. Tecumseh traveled tirelessly, urging Indian tribes across the nation to unite against whites. Tecumseh's Indian federation put up a heroic struggle, but could not hold out against the vast, well-armed American militia.

By the 1820s, Americans wanted all Indian land in the eastern United States. President Andrew Jackson signed the Indian Removal Act in 1830, which called for eastern tribes to be moved west of the Mississippi River to "Indian Territory" in Oklahoma. No tribes were spared. Even the Cherokee, Chickasaw, Choctaw, Creek, and Seminole nations—often called the "Five Civilized Tribes" by whites—were forced to go. The Choctaw, from the southern United States, went first. In 1831, two-thirds of the 20,000-member tribe left their homes on

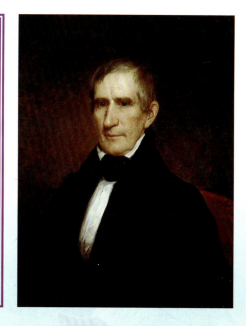

☞ William Henry Harrison was a stout believer in the concept of Manifest Destiny. This was the idea that Americans of European descent were destined to rule North America from the Atlantic to the Pacific. This theory overlooked the fact that the western lands were already occupied.

horseback, in wagons, and on foot, conducted by armed American soldiers. Along the way, freezing weather, pneumonia, cholera, and despair killed 2,000 Choctaw. The remaining Choctaw refused to go, so whites beat them, burned their homes, and destroyed their property. This procedure was repeated with tribe after tribe. One of the saddest events of this period was the Cherokee's trek from Georgia to Indian Territory in 1838. The Cherokee, forced to migrate along a route that is now called the "Trail of Tears," lost 4,000 people—almost one-quarter of their tribe—along the way. By the mid-1800s, more than 100,000 eastern Indians, from almost 30 tribes, had been moved across the Mississippi River.

While some Americans flocked to Indian lands in the east, others turned their gaze west. Whites headed to Oregon, Texas, and California—especially after gold was found there in 1848. As settlers kept moving west, the government continued to make treaties with Native American tribes. As before, tribes exchanged their property for money and promises of new land, food, blankets, and other supplies.

Commissioner of Indian Affairs George W. Manypenny protested white treatment of Indians. In 1856, he wrote: "Trespasses and depredations of every conceivable kind have been committed on the Indians. They have been personally maltreated, their property stolen, their timber destroyed, their possessions encroached upon, and diverse other wrongs and injuries done them."

AMERICA ESTABLISHES INDIAN TERRITORY

Despite the objections of Commissioner Manypenny and other concerned citizens, the federal government refused to stop land-grabbing settlers. The wide open stretches of land that lay to the west seemed like a dream come true to many white settlers. But the growing westward expansion would prove to be a nightmare for Native Americans.

👉 The Peace Commission, pictured here, met with Cheyenne and Arapaho Indians to end Red Cloud's War, a conflict the Indians were winning. The resulting treaty yielded the Powder River Valley and the Black Hills to the Native Americans—a promise that was broken within the next few years.

THE LAST INDIAN UPRISINGS

THE CIVIL WAR, WHICH LASTED FROM 1861 TO 1865, DISTRACTED MANY AMERICANS FROM THEIR conflict with the Indians. Some Native American leaders took advantage of the war and urged their followers to rise up against whites. Among the first to revolt were Sioux Indians that had been confined to a small reservation in Minnesota. Thirteen hundred braves, led by Chief Little Crow, launched a bloody uprising against white settlers.

But Americans quashed the rebellion, confiscated the Sioux's Minnesota land, and forced the Indians to move to the Dakota Territory. During the next quarter-century, almost all remaining "free" tribes were driven from their land and forced onto reservations.

In the early 1860s, the Mescalero Apache of New Mexico, who frequently raided white settlements, were pursued by Union General James Carleton and his troops. Overpowered, the Mescaleros surrendered and were relocated to a reservation called Bosque Redondo in central New Mexico.

22 LIFE ON THE RESERVATION

When General James Carleton gave orders to his soldiers, he said: "There is to be no council with the Indians, nor any talks. The men are to be slain whenever and wherever they can be found."

Carleton then decided to remove the Navajo from the Rio Grande Valley. After a brutal six-month campaign, during which Union soldiers killed Navajo Indians, burned their homes, and destroyed their crops and livestock, the Indians gave up. Thousands of Navajo were forcefully moved to Bosque Redondo.

Carleton planned to make Bosque Redondo a model reservation. He hoped to teach the Native Americans to be "civilized" Christian farmers who could grow their own food. Until the tribes were self-sufficient, the federal government would send food and supplies.

None of this turned out as Carleton hoped. Though some Indians planted crops, they had poor soil, few tools, little water, and no enthusiasm. The crops failed again and again. Meanwhile, dishonest suppliers sent rotten food for the hungry Indians. Moreover, living conditions at Bosque Redondo were squalid, drinking water was filthy, fuel was scarce, and illnesses were rampant. The Native Americans were used to an active life hunting game and gathering wild foods. They hated the reservation, and many sneaked away and clashed with white settlers. Carleton ordered the **fugitives** shot on sight.

THE LAST INDIAN UPRISINGS

👉 Chief Joseph of the Wallowa tribe of the Nez Perce tried to lead his people to Canada when the settlers drove them from their ancestral land in Oregon. Although they were captured at the border and forced to return to a reservation, the Americans respected his military leadership and dubbed him 'the Indian Napoleon.'

The federal government finally investigated Bosque Redondo in the late 1860s. As a result, 7,000 Navajo were released in 1868, and allowed to move to a reservation near their native land.

But the Indians' tragic story continued in other parts of the country. When gold was discovered in the Oregon

LIFE ON THE RESERVATION

Geronimo (1829–1909), leader of the Chiricahua Apache, boldly attacked colonists—both Mexican and American—in the Apache's southwestern territory. Geronimo was so successful in battle that some settlers claimed he had magical powers and was resistant to bullets.

American soldiers pursued Geronimo for 10 years, until 1884, when the Apache surrendered. Geronimo farmed for a short time on a reservation, then fled the reservation once more. United States troops again chased Geronimo, until March 1886, when he and his followers surrendered in Sonora, Mexico. As the Apache were being returned to the United States, Geronimo—afraid he would be murdered—again bolted.

At least 5,000 white soldiers and 500 Indian aides were then sent to track Geronimo to his hideout in the Sonora mountains. Geronimo surrendered for the last time in September 1886. He was imprisoned in Florida until 1894, then moved to Fort Sill in Oklahoma Territory. Geronimo died on February 17, 1909.

territory of the Nez Perce Indians in 1863, the American government demanded the land. The Nez Perce leader, Chief Joseph, resisted, but in 1877 the tribe was forced to move. As they left, three angry braves killed a group of white settlers.

THE LAST INDIAN UPRISINGS

Fearful of reprisals, the Nez Perce headed for Canada. For three months, American troops chased the Nez Perce as they trekked 1,000 miles north. Finally, the army surrounded the Indians in the Bear Paw Mountains, less than 40 miles from the Canadian border. After a five-day-battle, Chief Joseph surrendered. The Nez Perce were sent to a reservation in Indian Territory, where many got sick and died. In 1885—after Chief Joseph appealed to the federal government—the Nez Perce were permitted to move to a reservation in Washington, close to their ancestral home.

When Chief Joseph surrendered, on October 4, 1877, he uttered the following famous words: "I am tired of fighting... I want to have time to look for my children and see how many I can find. Maybe I shall find them among the dead. From where the sun now stands I will fight no more forever."

In 1867, Congress formed a "Peace Commission" to negotiate with hostile Indians. One of the commission's goals was to place all tribes east of the Rocky Mountains on reservations so located that they did not interfere with planned railroads. These reservations were intended to have land suitable for crops or grazing, so the Indians could support themselves. Negotiators offered Indians protection, food, and supplies if they moved to the chosen areas. Again and again, the government arranged for Native Americans to

LIFE ON THE RESERVATION

One American who protested white treatment of Indians was Senator Lot M. Morrill from Maine. In the 1860s, he declared: "We have come to this point in the history of the country that there is no place beyond population to which you can remove the Indian, and the precise question is: Will you exterminate him or will you fix an abiding (permanent) place for him?"

give up their land and move to reservations.

Many Indians refused to cooperate with the Peace Commission. Independent bands of Sioux, Arapaho, and Cheyenne continued attacking whites across the Great Plains. Union General William Tecumseh Sherman, sent to subdue the Indians, declared: "The more [Indians] we can kill this year, the less will have to be killed in the next war…They all have to be killed or be maintained as a species of paupers."

One of the keenest Indian fighters under Sherman's command was George Armstrong Custer. In 1874, when gold was discovered in the Black Hills of South Dakota, the sacred land of the Sioux, American miners, merchants, and settlers hurried to the region. The government offered to buy the land, but the Sioux refused to sell and prepared for war. On June 25, 1876, General Custer and 600 soldiers planned to attack an Indian camp along the Little Bighorn River. The Indians were ready. More than 2,500 Sioux braves, led by Chiefs Sitting Bull, Crazy Horse, and Rain-in-the-

THE LAST INDIAN UPRISINGS

> Sitting Bull (1831–1890) was chief of the Teton Sioux of the Great Plains. For much of his life, Sitting Bull led Sioux efforts to keep the United States from taking Indian land. After he and his warriors won the battle of the Little Bighorn, however, they still could not stop whites from settling in Sioux territory and wiping out buffalo herds. The resulting famine led Sitting Bull to surrender in 1881. After being a prisoner for two years, Sitting Bull was sent to live on the Standing Rock Reservation on the North Dakota-South Dakota border. He was released in 1885 and toured with the Buffalo Bill Wild West Show. In 1889, Sitting Bull returned to the reservation, where he spread the Ghost Dance religion. Fearing rebellion by Ghost Dance believers, authorities arrested Sitting Bull on December 15, 1890. Sitting Bull's followers tried to rescue him, and in the following gun battle, an Indian policeman shot and killed the great chief.

Face—along with thousands of warriors from other tribes—swooped down on Custer. The American soldiers fought bravely, but within 30 minutes, Custer and 225 of his men lay dead.

After the Native American victory at Little Bighorn, furious whites demanded that the government solve the "Indian problem" once and for all. American soldiers relentlessly hunted down Cheyenne, Sioux, and Apache Indians across the Great Plains. By the end of 1877, most of the Cheyenne and Sioux had surrendered and moved to reservations. Chief Sitting Bull and his Sioux band gave up in 1881. In the southwest, the Apaches led by Geronimo surrendered in 1886.

28 LIFE ON THE RESERVATION

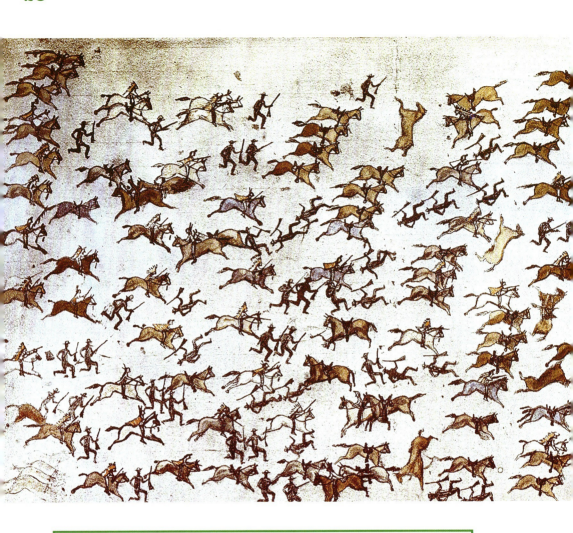

🍃 This Sioux drawing shows the chaotic fighting at the battle of the Little Bighorn. The defeat of George Custer's Seventh Cavalry by an overwhelming force of Sioux and Cheyenne warriors marked a high point for the Native Americans in their wars against U.S. expansion. After the battle, the military increased its efforts to force the Indians off their land. By 1890, nearly all of the Native Americans had been moved to reservations.

THE LAST INDIAN UPRISINGS

In 1890, the final shots were fired in the Indian Wars. The U.S. government had become concerned about a new religion that was becoming popular among the Great Plains Indians. They feared this Ghost Dance religion would lead to uprisings, so soldiers were sent to control the situation. In December 1890, when 350 Sioux men, women, and children fled from the Cheyenne River Reservation to the Pine Ridge Reservation, 150 miles away, American soldiers chased them. The U.S. troops forced the travelers into an army camp at Wounded Knee Creek. The next morning, as soldiers were taking the Indians' weapons, a scuffle broke out. Soldiers opened fire with machine guns, and killed 290 unarmed Sioux. With the massacre at Wounded Knee, the Indian uprisings in the United States had come to an end. Native Americans had given up hope.

The Ghost Dance religion foretold the arrival of an Indian messiah who would cast out whites and restore Indian land and culture.

🔥 The general store and post office on a reservation in New Mexico is shown here. The Native Americans' newfound reliance on white ways became a means by which the U.S. government could control more aspects of their lives.

RESERVATIONS

BY THE LATE 1800S, ALMOST ALL NATIVE AMERICANS HAD BEEN MOVED TO RESERVATIONS. Though the government created most reservations on land that whites did not want, Indians were expected to build homes there, establish farms, raise livestock, and provide for themselves—an almost impossible task. The Bureau of Indian Affairs, formed to help Native Americans, did a poor job. The government did not provide enough food, clothing, farm equipment, seeds, cattle, guns for hunting game, tools, or other supplies. Some Indians tried to farm, but they were unsuccessful because they lacked proper implements—and they were weakened by malnutrition and disease. To make matters worse, the government did not keep white settlers off Indian reservations, where whites grazed cattle, searched for minerals, cut trees, and built railroads.

Railroads were disastrous for Indians. Railroad tracks cut across reservations, upset Native American communities, and disturbed animal **migration** patterns. Trains also brought more whites, who hunted buffalo almost to **extinction**. The buffalo were vital to the Plains Indians' way of life. Buffalo meat provided food; buffalo skin was made into clothing, shoes, water buckets, blankets, and tepee

32 LIFE ON THE RESERVATION

Faced with reservation life, Chief Satanta of the Kiowa declared: "I love the land and the buffalo and will not part with it…I want the children raised as I was. I have heard that you want to settle us on a reservation near the [Wichita] mountains. I don't want to settle. I love to roam over the prairies. There I feel free and happy, but when I settle down I feel pale and die."

coverings; and buffalo bones were used for tools. Confined to poor land and deprived of the ability to fend for themselves, Native Americans had to rely on the government to provide the necessities of life.

Meanwhile, ever since their first contact with Native Americans, most whites had considered the Indian culture to be less valuable than their own. Some whites even felt the Native American way of life was sinful. Once reservations were well established, white teachers, administrators, and preachers rushed in to change Indian customs. The government prohibited Indian names, clothing, dances, songs, and hairstyles, and discouraged Indians from using their native language. Indians who had several wives were ordered to break up their extra marriages—without regard to the effect on families.

Americans then tried to impose white culture on Native Americans. This was shattering for tribes because white values are different from Indian values. Indians have a spiritual attachment to their land, and generally do not strive

🔥 This group of Chiracahua Apache Indian children was photographed on their first day at Carlisle Indian school, and again after four months of attendance. Their appearance is markedly more Americanized, including haircuts and tighter-fitting clothes. 🔥

LIFE ON THE RESERVATION

Satanta (1820–1878) was a chief of the Kiowa Indians, who lived on the Great Plains. In 1867, the Kiowa were pushed off their land by whites and forced to live on a reservation in Oklahoma. Determined to regain freedom for his tribe, Satanta left the reservation and plundered white settlements. He was forced back to the reservation in 1869, but left again in early 1871.

Satanta then led another series of raids, during which many Texans were killed. Satanta was arrested in June 1871, tried in Texas, and sentenced to hang. Fearing revenge from the Kiowa, the Texas governor paroled Satanta in October 1873—with the condition that the Kiowa stay on their reservation. Satanta ignored this provision and immediately renewed his attacks on whites.

In 1874, after many whites were killed, thousands of American troops stormed Satanta and his comrades in the Red River Valley of Texas. After 14 fierce battles, the Indians surrendered. Satanta was arrested again and sent to the Texas State Penitentiary. In October 1874, depressed by the idea of spending the rest of his life in prison, Satanta killed himself by jumping out a window.

to gain property, riches, and power for themselves. Instead, they share goods and duties with tribe members. Also, Indians do not have the same attitude toward work as whites. Native

RESERVATIONS 35

Americans work to provide food, clothing, and shelter, but they also savor free time to enjoy nature, life, and beauty. Unfortunately, many whites thought this meant Indians were lazy. Whites also took away the Native Americans' sacred instruments, medicines, and pipes, and tried to change Indians' religious beliefs—which include dreams, visions, myths, talking animals, magic, and ceremonies.

When told to dissolve all but one of his marriages, Comanche Chief Quanah Parker demanded: "You talk about wives. Which one I throw away? You pick him? You little girl, you go 'way; you got no papa—you pick him? You little fellow, you go 'way; you got no papa—you pick him?"

When Native Americans resisted these changes, the government imprisoned them, forced them to do hard labor, and deprived them of food. The result of these policies was to weaken Indian families, damage Indian culture, and drive Indians to despair.

The American government set up day schools and boarding schools for Indian youngsters. Often, Indian children were taken from their tribes, sent to live at white boarding schools, forbidden to use their native language, and taught white culture. This attempt to "make Indians white" was tragic for Native Americans. Families were ripped apart, and many Native American children grew up unable to adjust to either

LIFE ON THE RESERVATION

George E. Ellis, a Massachusetts clergyman, defended white policy toward reservation Indians. In 1882, he wrote: "We have a full right…to dictate terms and conditions to them…to say…what they must and shall do… The Indian must be made to feel he is in the grasp of a superior."

the Indian or white world.

American officials recognized that the Indians had problems. They wanted Native Americans to become less dependent on federal aid. To accomplish this, Congress passed the Dawes Act in 1887. This law "allotted," or gave, sections of land to individual Indians rather than to the tribe as a whole. Indians were then expected to become independent farmers and grow food for themselves and to sell. Officials hoped this would help Native Americans earn money and blend into the white world.

The Dawes Act was a disaster for Native Americans. Many Indian men would not farm because their culture considered this woman's work, not suitable for hunters and warriors. Other Indians tried to grow crops but failed. As a result, whites were able to trick many Indians into selling their land.

The situation worsened in the 1900s. During World War I, which lasted from 1914 to 1918, food was needed for American troops. Indians, therefore, were pressured to sell their land to white farmers. After the war, America's population grew, more people moved west, and whites continued to prod Indians into selling their property. By 1934, two-thirds of all Indians either had no land or too little land to make a living. The Dawes Act resulted in the Indians becoming more dependent on the government—exactly the opposite of what it had intended.

The terrible consequences of the Dawes Act convinced many Americans to demand changes in Indian policy. Indian supporters wanted a program that would keep reservations whole, preserve Native American culture, and give Indians the same rights as other citizens. In 1934 Congress passed the Indian Reorganization Act. This law stopped allotment, regulated sale of Indian lands, and gave back some tribal property. It also

> In 1924 all the Native Americans in the United States were made citizens. This meant they were entitled to the same rights and privileges as other American citizens. However, the Native Americans who are members of tribes that the government recognizes have a special status. Because their tribes are political entities, they are not subject to certain state laws. The tribes have the power to tax tribe members, to issue charters, to regulate marriage and divorce, and to make certain laws. This authority is recognized by the federal government and by the individual states. Some tribes even have the right to conduct all civil trials and most criminal trials (except for major crimes like murder or arson).

provided funds for new clinics, roads, schools, community centers, and **irrigation** systems on reservations. Moreover, Native Americans were permitted to govern themselves and encouraged to become economically independent.

By the 20th century, most Native Americans followed both Indian and white customs. For example, Indians combined the old ways, like hunting and gathering, with trips to the store; sick Indians sought help from both **medicine men** and doctors; Native Americans spoke their tribal language as well as English. When Indian soldiers returned from World War I, they were greeted with **purification rights** and celebration feasts, like warriors of past times. And though some Indians—like the Osage—had comfortable houses, they followed the Indian tradition of visiting friends and relatives for months at a time.

When World War II began in 1939, it affected all Americans, including Indians. Native Americans left reservations in droves, some to join the army, others to work in **defense plants** and factories. After the war, some Native Americans did not return to the reservations. Instead, they lived and worked in cities, among whites.

The success of a number of Indians during World War II convinced Congress that Native Americans could now take care of themselves. The government began "terminating" tribes in 1953. When a tribe was **terminated**, its members could sell their land and divide up the money. The Indians were then expected to move to **urban** areas and get jobs. The

RESERVATIONS

termination act was another disaster for Native Americans. It broke up reservations, destroyed tribes, and left Indians with few resources and little power.

In 1957, Congress stopped termination unless a tribe requested it. By this time, Indians were voting in large numbers, and lawmakers feared Native Americans would vote against politicians that opposed Indian reforms.

The tension between white Americans and Native Americans continued to exist. Americans needed to change the attitudes that had shaped government policies for centuries.

After the Dawes Act failed, a Sioux man observed: "We Indians will be Indians all our lives, we never will be white men. We can talk and work and go to school like the white people but we're still Indians."

💧 A man garbed in full Indian dress dances as part of a protest at the Capitol building in Washington, D.C. Native Americans have raised their voices in recent years, opposing policies that work against them or overlook their needs.

CHANGES ON THE RESERVATIONS

IN 1961, NATIVE AMERICAN LEADERS PUT FORTH A "DECLARATION OF INDIAN PURPOSE," THAT called for the government to give back lost reservations, restore Indian freedom and rights, and improve the lives of Native Americans. Indians also protested and **demonstrated**, to pressure lawmakers into meeting their demands. Two famous demonstrations occurred at Alcatraz Island in San Francisco Bay during the late 1960s and at the town of Wounded Knee in South Dakota in 1973. These protests forced the government to respond to the Indians' plight. New programs were started, such as Head Start (early education) for Indian children and grants and loans for public improvement projects.

Lyndon Johnson, who was president from 1963 to 1969, supported new Indian policies and improvements on reservations, including construction of roads, water lines, and sewer lines. President Richard Nixon, in office from 1969 to 1974, also helped Native Americans. During his administration, additional Indian land was returned, Indian tribes were given

Names associated with Native Americans, like "Braves," "Chiefs," "Indians," "Redskins," "Squaws," "Tomahawks," "Warriors", "Fighting Sioux," and so on, are commonly used for school and professional sports teams. Many Native Americans find this offensive. W. Ron Allen, president of the National Congress of American Indians, said: "The National Congress of American Indians strongly condemns the use of sports team mascots…It is a national insult and does nothing to honor the Native peoples of this country."

more power to govern themselves, and funds were provided to improve schools, legal aid, and medical clinics on reservations. Nevertheless, many tribes continued to need government aid.

During the presidency of Ronald Reagan, from 1981 to 1989, federal budget cuts compelled tribes to find ways to generate jobs and income. Native Americans became better at fund-raising and at drawing attention to their needs. When President Bill Clinton took office in 1993, he worked to increase tribal power and speed up economic development on reservations.

In the last part of the 20th century, new government programs gave tribes loans to start businesses. Some Indians developed natural resources on their land, such as timber, coal, oil, and minerals. The Cherokee Nation built motels, gift shops, a ranch, a lumber company, a greenhouse business, and factories that manufacture cables and fiber optic equipment; some tribes

CHANGES ON THE RESERVATIONS

👆 Indian activist Russell Means raises his handcuffed fist after being arrested for blocking a Columbus Day parade. Because of their perspective on American history, many Native Americans do not believe a celebration of Christopher Columbus is warranted.

run hotels with conference centers and recreation areas; others have plants that make mirrors, tank accessories, or car parts; and many Indians make and sell crafts, including jewelry, artwork, rugs, clothes, baskets, beaded pouches, quilts, wood carvings, and embroidered jackets. The Navajo

44 LIFE ON THE RESERVATION

👆 This picture, taken in 1988, shows then-president Ronald Reagan meeting with Native American leaders. Seated on his left is Wilma Mankiller, principal chief of the Cherokee Nation.

in particular are skilled silversmiths and weavers, and their rugs, silver and turquoise jewelry, and silver ornaments are very popular. In the 1980s, some tribes started building gambling casinos on their reservations, with bingo, blackjack, roulette tables, slot machines, and other games. Though some people object to casinos on moral grounds, many Native Americans think they provide badly needed jobs and money.

Large numbers of Indians have moved to cities. This trend began earlier in the 20th century for a number of reasons: most reservation Indians were unemployed and poor; young

CHANGES ON THE RESERVATIONS

Russell Means, an Oglala Sioux Indian, was born in 1939 on the Pine Ridge Reservation in South Dakota. He grew up in California, where he had a difficult early life and became an alcoholic. In the late 1960s Means settled down and joined the American Indian Movement (AIM), a civil rights organization that sought to restore Indian land and rights.

In 1972, Means led the "Trail of Broken Treaties" march on Washington, to demand that the government honor past treaties with Indians. Means and the AIM also seized files from the Bureau of Indian Affairs; these showed that the government had wrongly taken Indian territory. In 1973, Means led AIM's 71-day siege at Wounded Knee—where American troops had massacred Indians in 1890—to protest a corrupt Sioux tribal government and get back land that was promised to the Sioux.

In the early 1970s, Means got into trouble with the law, was tried for murder, and found not guilty. In the 1980s, Means ran for vice-president and president, to focus public attention on Indian problems. Over the years Means had many differences with the AIM, and permanently resigned in 1988.

Besides being an Indian activist, Means is an actor, writer, and musician. He has had roles on television and in movies, including *The Last of the Mohicans*, *Natural Born Killers*, and *Pocahontas* (as the voice of Powhatan). Means also published his autobiography, *Where White Men Fear to Tread*, which discusses his troubled life and his dedication to Native American causes. Means' music albums also reflect his struggle for Indian rights.

Indians were encouraged to become working Americans; and tribes were being "terminated." Job-seeking Native Americans flocked to Denver, Detroit, Los Angeles, Minneapolis, New

> Wilma Mankiller, a Cherokee Indian, was born in 1945 and grew up on Mankiller Flats—her family's farm in Oklahoma. When the farm failed in 1956, Mankiller's family moved to California as part of the government's Indian relocation program. There, Mankiller studied sociology and got a job as a social worker. Mankiller became involved in the struggle for Indian rights in the late 1960s.
>
> In the 1970s, Mankiller moved back to Oklahoma to reclaim Mankiller Flats. She got a job with the Cherokee Nation, and started several projects to help Indians get jobs and homes. Mankiller served as chief of the Cherokee Nation from 1985 until 1995. She was the first woman chief of a major Indian tribe. "Prior to my election," said Mankiller, "young Cherokee girls would never have thought that they might grow up and become chief."
>
> In 1986 Mankiller was named American Indian Woman of the Year by the Oklahoma Federation of Indian Women, and was inducted into the Oklahoma Hall of Fame. Mankiller was admitted to the National Women's Hall of Fame in 1993, and honored by Oklahoma's Institute of Indian Heritage in 1994. Mankiller describes her life and work in her autobiography, *Mankiller: A Chief and Her People*.

York, Phoenix, San Francisco, Seattle, and other cities.

Sadly, this led to massive culture shock. Most Indians had never seen a large city, with skyscrapers, traffic jams, and millions of people packed into rows of houses. Native Americans were unfamiliar with sidewalks, subways, buses, and supermarkets. They were not accustomed to going to work and eating meals "by the clock." Furthermore, most Indians had

CHANGES ON THE RESERVATIONS

little or no job training, and could not get decent employment. Urban Indians, therefore, usually ended up in crowded **ghettoes**, with no money and little hope for the future.

Fortunately, this situation is improving as reservations become more prosperous, and Native Americans become better educated and trained for various jobs. But the American nation still needs to seek new ways to heal the old wounds left by reservations' long and painful history.

👆 Representatives from over 700 tribes from the North American continent assemble at the Annual Gathering of Nations Powwow in New Mexico. Over 3,000 Indian dancers meet here to socialize and compete each year.

MODERN RESERVATIONS

AT THE PRESENT TIME, THERE ARE ALMOST 300 RESERVATIONS IN THE UNITED STATES. THOUGH reservations are no longer permanent homes for many Indians, they continue to be an important part of Native American identity. The largest is the 17-million-acre Navajo Reservation, which covers parts of Arizona, New Mexico, and Utah. Other reservations are scattered from Maine to California, and range in size from the Papago Reservation in Arizona, which contains about 41,600 acres, to the one-acre Strawberry Valley Rancheria in California.

Indian Reservations are similar to other American communities in many ways. They usually have at least one town, with government offices, a gas station, a bank, a grocery store, and other small businesses. Most people on reservations can speak English and are familiar with American culture through television, radio, magazines, newspapers, and movies.

Reservations usually have various types of homes, ranging from houses to huts, tents, and tepees. The traditional Navajo dwelling, for example, is the hogan—a dome-shaped structure with six or eight sides, made of logs covered with earth.

50 LIFE ON THE RESERVATION

Most people are aware that English words like mocassin, papoose, tomahawk, wampum, and wigwam were first spoken by Native Americans. Other common words that come from Indian languages are barbecue, buccaneer, cannibal, hammock, hurricane, iguana, muck-a-muck ("big shot"), opossum, pecan, persimmon, raccoon, squash (the vegetable), tobacco, toboggan, and woodchuck.

Because many reservation Indians are poor, two or three families often share a home, and crowding is common. Many reservations also have poor sanitation and sewage disposal. This is expected to improve, though, as the people living on the reservations improve their standards of living.

Education has become important to many Native Americans. Classes about Native American culture, which teach the tribe's language, ancestral arts and crafts, history, and traditions, have been added to the curriculum in many reservation schools. In addition, an increasing number of Indians are going to college and becoming teachers, lawyers, doctors, engineers, and other professionals.

Religion is also an important factor in Native Americans' growing sense of identity. Their religious faith includes deep respect for trees, stones, rivers, animals, mountains, caves, and other parts of nature. Most Indians have become Christians over the past two centuries, and the Native American Church

MODERN RESERVATIONS

▶ A cashier changes money for gamblers at the Casino Sandia, on Sandia Pueblo in New Mexico. Although the ethics of casinos are sometimes questioned, they are a vital source of employment and income for Native Americans today.

combines Christianity with traditional Indian beliefs and customs—such as the use of peyote (a drug that causes visions) to communicate with God. In addition, renewed pride in their heritage has brought many Indians back to their ancestral religions.

The Indian Health Services, a federal agency, provides medical care for reservation Indians. Many Native Americans also consult a shaman or medicine man when they are ill. Medicine men use prayer, fasting, herbs, sweathouses (saunas),

LIFE ON THE RESERVATION

> Susan LaFlesche Picotte (1865–1915), an Omaha Indian, was born on the Omaha Reservation in Nebraska. As a child, Picotte attended reservation schools, then went on to schools in New Jersey and Virginia. Afterwards, Picotte enrolled at the Woman's Medical College of Pennsylvania. She graduated in 1889 and became the first female Native American doctor. A year later, Picotte returned to her reservation and provided health care for her tribe. In 1894 Picotte married and settled in Bancroft, Nebraska, where she doctored both Indians and whites.
>
> Picotte was among the first residents of the town of Walthill when it was founded on the Omaha Reservation in 1906. There, she was chairman of the local board of health, established a hospital, worked to prohibit the sale of alcohol, and became a respected Omaha leader. Picotte was comfortable with white culture, but she never lost touch with her Indian heritage. When Picotte died, a Christian clergyman conducted her funeral, but the closing prayer was made in the Omaha language by a Native American.

and medicine chants to cure their patients. The Navajo, for example, believe all illnesses have supernatural causes. To cure a sick Navajo, therefore, a shaman performs a "sing." During this ceremony, performed in a Navajo home, the patient's friends and relatives join the shaman in chants.

Alcoholism is the most widespread medical problem among Native Americans today. For this reason, health care workers have instituted prevention programs in schools and community centers. These programs warn Native Americans about the dangers of alcohol. Treatment centers are also

MODERN RESERVATIONS

available on some reservations.

Most Indians still combine new ways with old traditions. The Chippewa on the Red Lake Indian Reservation in Minnesota, for instance, watch Viking football games on television, own cars, and live in traditional American homes. They also smoke fish over open fires, harvest wild rice, and have religious ceremonies led by a shaman, as their ancestors did.

Sadly, much Indian culture has been lost. Indians across the country, though, are working to save their traditions, customs, and language. Tribes, for example, periodically have **powwows**. These festivities bring Indians together for athletic events, games, discussions, feasts, and dancing. Indians engage in many kinds of dances—for new seasons, religious observances, remembrances of past times, and other celebrations.

Indian artists, athletes, dancers, singers, and writers bloomed in the 20th century. Examples are the writers James Welch, Leslie Marmon Silko, Louise Eldrich, Michael Dorris,

Many names on the U.S. map have Indian names.
States: the Dakotas, Illinois, Iowa, Kansas, Massachusetts, Missouri, Ohio, and Oklahoma.
Cities: Chicago, Omaha, Miami, Seattle, Seneca, Sheboygan, Topeka, and Wichita.
Lakes: Michigan, Oneida, Winnebago, and Okeechobee.
Rivers: Mississippi, Potomac, Apalachicola, and Chattahoochee.
Bays: Chesapeake, Narragansett, and Pascagoula.

Jim Thorpe (1888–1953), an Indian of Sauk and Fox ancestry, was born in Oklahoma and attended Haskell Indian School in Kansas and Carlisle Indian School in Pennsylvania. Thorpe played semi-professional baseball in 1909 and 1910, was on All-American Football teams in 1911 and 1912, and won Olympic gold medals for the decathlon and pentathlon in 1912. The Olympic medals were taken away in 1913 because Thorpe had been a "professional" baseball player, but they were later returned to his family.

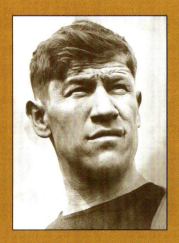

Thorpe played on National Baseball League teams from 1913 to 1919, was a professional football star from 1915 to 1929, and excelled in archery, basketball, boxing, hockey, lacrosse, swimming, and tennis. In 1950, American sports writers and broadcasters selected Thorpe as the greatest American athlete and the greatest football player of the first half of the 20th century.

After he retired from sports, Thorpe had small parts in movies, lectured about American Indian culture, and was a seaman with the United States Merchant Marine. To honor Thorpe, Pennsylvania formed the borough of Jim Thorpe in 1954.

and Sherman Alexie; the ballerinas Maria and Marjorie Tallchief; Olympic Gold Medal winner Jim Thorpe; artist R.C. Gorman; and folk singer Buffy Sainte-Marie.

MODERN RESERVATIONS

There were about one million Indians in North America when European colonists arrived in the 1600s. By 1890, only 240,000 native Americans remained. Today, because of higher birth rates, better health care, and improved nutrition, North America is home to about two million Indians. With government assistance, better social and economic conditions, and increased education, life on and off the reservation should continue to improve for Native Americans.

GLOSSARY

Colonizing
The act of sending a group of people to a new land or region to settle.

Defense plants
Factories that manufacture arms, ammunition, and other equipment used to fight a war.

Demonstrated
Made a public display of group feelings in support or opposition of a specific cause.

Extinction
When a species no longer exists.

Fugitives
Runaways or refugees.

Ghettoes
The areas of a city where minority groups live because they lack money to live elsewhere.

Irrigation
A system for supplying land with water through manmade means.

Medicine men
Native American healers.

Migrants
People who move from place to place.

GLOSSARY

Migration
The pattern of moving regularly from one area to another.

Negotiator
A person who helps settle controversies.

Nomadic
Roaming from place to place without any particular pattern.

Powwow
A traditional Native American ceremony featuring dance, feasting and a blessing by religious leaders. Powwows were often held before a major hunt or as part of a gathering of tribes.

Purification rights
Ceremonies used to make a person spiritually and physically clean.

Reservation
Land set aside by the U.S. government for Native Americans.

Superintendent
An executive; a person who is in charge of an organization.

Terminated
Ended.

Urban
City-like.

TIMELINE

20,000-60,000 years ago
Ancestors of Native Americans cross a land bridge from Asia to North America. Over time they spread across the continent and give rise to numerous Indian tribes.

1607
The first British colony is founded in Jamestown, Virginia.

1620
English Puritans found Plymouth, Massachusetts.

1600s
Whites swarm over Indian land on the East Coast. Eastern tribes fight colonists and lose.

1754–1763
The French and Indian War is fought. Britain wins, and seizes French territory west of the Appalachian Mountains.

Late 1700s
British colonists overcome Indian resistance and move west of the Appalachian mountains.

1776–1783
American War of Independence is fought. America wins and extends its boundaries. Colonists take over more Indian land.

1787
Congress passes an ordinance that allows Americans to settle the Northwest Territory.

Early 1800s
American settlers overcome Indian resistance and pour into the Northwest Territory.

1830
President Andrew Jackson signs the Indian Removal Act that calls for eastern tribes to be moved to "Indian Territory" in Oklahoma. Many tribes are forced to relocate.

1848
Gold is discovered in California. Whites flock west and move onto Indian land displacing the California Indians.

1861–1865
Americans fight the Civil War. Some tribes take the opportunity to rise up against whites but are defeated.

1867
Congress forms the "Peace Commission" to convince Great Plains Indians to move to reservations. Many tribes resist.

1876
General George Armstrong Custer and his troops are killed at the battle of Little Bighorn.

1876–1886
American troops hunt down Great Plains Indians and force them onto reservations. Americans try to impose white culture on Indians.

1887
Congress passes the Dawes Act that "allots" land to individual Indians rather than to tribes as a whole. The project is a disaster for Indians.

1914–1918
America fights in World War I. Troops need food so Indians are pressured to sell their land to white farmers.

1934
Congress passes the Indian Reorganization Act; this stops allotment and gives Native Americans more rights.

1939–1945
America is involved in World War II. Indians join the army and work in factories. After the war, some Indians remain in cities.

1953
The government begins "terminating" tribes. Native Americans are expected to move to cities and get jobs. The project is a disaster for Indians.

LIFE ON THE RESERVATION

1957
Congress stops termination unless a tribe requests it.

1961
Native American leaders publish a "Declaration of Indian Purpose," that calls for the government to give back lost reservations and restore Indian rights. Indians begin demonstrating to demand changes.

1960s and 1970s
The government reforms its Indian policies.

1980s
Budget cuts require Indians to become more self-reliant.

1990s
The government speeds up economic development on reservations and gives tribal governments more power.

21st century
Native Americans demand more freedom and greater control over their land.

FURTHER READING

Ashabranner, Brent. *A Strange and Distant Shore: Indians of the Great Plains in Exile*. Brookfield, Conn.: Cobblehill Books, 1996.

Bol, Marsha C. *American Indians and the Natural World*. Niwot, Colo: Roberts Rinehart, 1998.

Dunn, John M. *The Relocation of the North American Indian*. San Diego: Lucent Books, 1995.

Marks, Paula Mitchell. *In a Barren Land: American Indian Dispossession and Survival*. New York, William Morrow, 1998.

Parchemin, Richard, ed. *The Life and History of North America's Indian Reservations*. London: Kiln House, 1998.

Perry, Richard J. *Apache Reservation: Indigenous Peoples and the American State*. Austin, University of Texas Press, 1993.

Smith, Carter, ed. *A Sourcebook on the American West: Native Americans of the West*. New York: Millbrook, 1992.

Viola, Herman J. *North American Indians: An Introduction to the Lives of America's Native Peoples, from the Inuit of the Arctic to the Zuni of the Southwest*. New York: Crown Publishers, 1996.

Important leaders of the 18th and 19th centuries

http://detnews.com/history/pontiac/pontiac.htm

http://www.tvdsb.on.ca/tecumseh/man/

http://www.pbs.org/weta/thewest/wpages/wpgs680/sbarrest.htm

http://www.desertusa.com/magfeb98/feb_pap/du_apache.htm

http://www.powersource.com/gallery/people/geronimo.html

http://www.i5ive.com/topic_page.cfm/5871/1367

http://www.tsha.utexas.edu/handbook/online/articles/view/SS/fsa33.html

http://www.incwell.com/Biographies/SittingBull.html

http://www.powersource.com/gallery/people/sittbull.html

Native American Literature

http://www.indigenouspeople.org/natlit/tecumseh.htm

Modern-day Native Leaders

http://www.ssa.gov/aian/wilma.htm

http://www.uic.edu/depts/owa/history_month_97/mankiller.html

http://www.russellmeans.com/current_03.html

http://www.geocities.com/Hollywood/Agency/6393/russellmeans.html

http://www.getmusic.com/artists/amg/Artist/227/169227.html

http://www.russellmeans.com/aim.html

INDEX

American Revolution, 15
Apache Indians, 7, 21, 27-29
Arapaho Indians, 7, 26

Bering Strait, 7
Blackfeet Indians, 7
Bosque Redondo, 21-23

Carleton, James, 21-22
Cherokee Indians, 17, 18, 42
Cheyenne Indians, 26, 27-29
Chicksaw Indians, 17
Chief Joseph, 24-25
Chippewa Indians, 53
Choctaw Indians, 7, 17-18
Clinton, Bill, 42
Comanche Indians, 7
Crazy Horse, 26
Creek Indians, 17
Custer, George Armstrong, 26-27

Dawes Act, 36-37
Declaration of Indian Purpose, 41
Delaware Indians, 7

Geronimo, 29

Harrison, William Henry, 16-17

Indian Health Services, 51
Indian Removal Act, 17
Indian Reorganization Act, 38
Iowa Indians, 7

Jackson, Andrew, 17
Jamestown, Virginia, 8
Johnson, Lyndon, 41

Kansa Indians, 7

Little Bighorn, battle of, 26-27
Little Crow, 21
Little Turtle, 15

Manypenny, George W., 18-19
Miami Indians, 15

Mississippi River, 16, 17
Mohave Indians, 7

Native American Church, 50-51
Native Americans
    conditions on reservations, 22, 31-39, 49-55
    effects of colonization on, 7-13, 27-29
    improvements for, 37-39, 41-44, 47
    mistreatment of, 8-13, 15, 16, 18, 22, 29, 31-37
Navajo Indians, 7, 22, 23, 49, 52
Nez Perce Indians, 24-25
Nixon, Richard, 41
Northwest Ordinance, 15

Omaha Indians, 7

Peace Commission, 25-26
Penn, William, 8
Powhatan Indians, 8

Rain-in-the-Face, 26
Reagan, Ronald, 42

Seminole Indians, 17
Shawnee Indians, 17
Sherman, William Tecumseh, 26
Sioux Indians, 21, 26, 27-29
Sitting Bull, 26, 29

Tecumseh, 17
Trail of Tears, 18

Williams, Roger, 8
World War I, 37
World War II, 38
Wounded Knee, 29, 41

Zuni Indians, 7

PHOTO CREDITS

2:	Bettmann/Corbis	30:	Hulton/Archive
6:	Francis G. Mayer/Corbis	33:	both Hulton/Archive
9:	National Park Service/Colonial National Historical Park	34:	Denver Public Library
		40:	Hulton/Archive
		43:	Hulton/Archive
10:	Hulton/Archive	44:	Bettmann/Corbis
11:	Hulton/Archive	48-49:	Hulton/Archive
14-15:	Corbis	51:	Miguel Gandert/Corbis
17:	Bettmann/Corbis	54:	Hulton/Archive
20-21:	National Archives		
23:	Hulton/Archive		
24:	Arizona Historical Society		
28-29:	Reproduced from *A Pictographic History of the Oglala Sioux*, by Amos Bad Heart Bull, text by Helen H. Blish, by permission of the University of Nebraska Press. Plate 182.		

Cover photos:
(front) Hulton/Archive
(back) Hulton/Archive

AUTHOR

Dr. Barbara Saffer, a former college instructor, holds Ph.D. degrees in biology and geology. She has written numerous books for young people about science, geography, exploration, and the American West. She lives in Birmingham, Alabama, with her family.

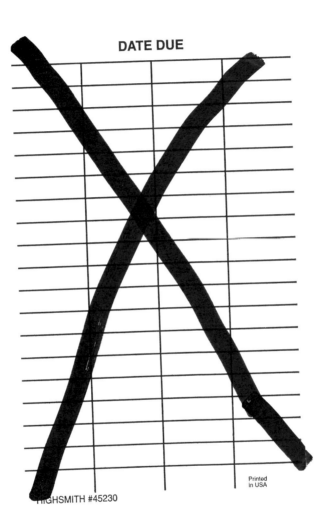